RAW BEAUTY

Smoothies, Shakes & Creamies

LAURIE VUKICH

DEDICATION

This book is dedicated to our family, whom we LOVE. We are thrilled to watch each of you make healthy changes so we can enjoy you longer, and to see the sparkle in your eyes as you are embracing better health! That is true happiness!

We also dedicate this book to our wonderful viewers at www.naturesknockout.com, whom we adore and share in your enthusiasm and applaud every step of your progress. Your support and enthusiasm keep us going, and fill our hearts with the utmost gratitude.

And to each of you, who want or need to get off sugar, gluten, dairy, soy, or chemicals, or just desire to feel better, and want to make the transition as painless and delicious as possible...

now you can do it!

disclaimer

The intent of this book is to be a source of information we've compiled in our personal journey for better health. It is not a medical commentary.

We avoid ingredients we feel to be toxic, however some of the ingredients in this book could cause allergic reactions for some. Please use caution and always consult a medical professional with any questions or before changing your diet or exercise routine. The use or misuse of any recipe or information in this book is at the reader's own risk and the writers and publishers cannot be held liable for any adverse reactions that may occur.

www.naturesknockout.com

TOOLS & EQUIPMENT

In this book, we'll show you how to make yogurt without an expensive yogurt maker, and do all we can to help make this transition to a wonderful new life simple and delicious.

So no need to go crazy buying unnecessary gadgets, but there are a few items that we'd suggest that you will want to pick up. If nothing else, make sure you have a great blender, it will make a world of difference immediately. It may seem expensive, but the money you save in the long run, will by far make it worth every penny or pound you shed.

Here are some basic equipment items that we recommend.

- VitaMix Blender or Blendtec
- Nut Milk Bag
- Glass Bowls
- Food Dehydrator
- Glasses to drink from
  (nothing plastic or silicone

contents

www.naturesknockout.com

WELCOME TO BOOK #2

We're so glad you're joining us in this journey! This book was designed to be the SECOND STEP in our Beauty Foods Series. If you started with our "Beauty In Every Bite Desserts" Cookbook (BOOK ONE), congratulations, you are on your way, and may even be completely off of refined sugar already. That's super exciting and you deserve to celebrate (not with sugar, of course!) But it makes us so happy to see you reaching toward a path that has brought us so much joy.

If you aren't off refined sugar yet, or if you didn't start with BOOK ONE, it's okay, we won't punish you. Although 25 extra pushups may not be a bad idea. :) But don't worry, because the sooner you get these smoothies and probiotics into your life, the better off you will be. The focus of BOOK ONE was to help you find amazing replacements as you got completely off refined sugar. The purpose of this book is to replenish and renew the body. The results tend to bring an even greater change to your skin, hair, nails, and of course, everything on the inside tends to do much better as well.

You're in for a lot of fun on this new journey and we've got more books coming, so we can be with you every step of the way, cheering you on!

Are you ready for some action?! Let's go!

rant & rave

I write this book with a heart so full of happiness that it just might pop. Not really, but that's just how I feel. Don't worry, we don't believe in doing anything to hurt our hearts, or any part of our bodies, for that matter. In fact we celebrate the wonder of our bodies and love that they respond so well when we nurture and care for them.

Back to my full heart, I have the best family in the world (sorry to all other families out there, j/k) but they have been beyond supportive and so encouraging of our website, books, speaking engagements, and everything we are doing to get the word out and to help everyone in this world feel and look better.

But I was afraid our works were falling on deaf ears, as our family members would nod at what we would share, then grab for a doughnut or other sinful item and indulge. We wanted more than anything for them to have at least 1 week of feeling amazing so they would never want to return to their old eating routines. But we would learn that what we wanted for them had to be what they wanted for themselves.

Probably the biggest opposition I received was from (yes) my sweet husband. I think the meanest thing a woman can do is to get between a man and his food.

But with our "foods" no longer consisting of food, and the occurrence of auto-immune disease, cancer, and autism being at an epidemic all time high, I wanted him to want to want to be more healthy and he just wasn't there yet.

I love that many studies are pointing to real foods...whole, organic, and non genetically modified (GMO) foods and showing that they can rebuild the body, accelerate recovery, and in some cases, have even sparked complete reversal of many diseases. That is exciting!

We believe firmly that changing our diets can improve the way we all feel, because we live it, our viewers live it, and they share inspiring and convincing testimonials with us all of the time.

8

After my daughter, Tiffany was diagnosed with a crippling autoimmune disease, we dug into intense, comprehensive research which led us down the path to the diet that we now share and literally thrive on.

TRENT & CAYDEN VUKICH

PHOTO BY: CAMI LOW

We've seen miracles take place. Our goal was to get Tiffany better, and she has improved, and can completely control her Rheumatoid Arthritis, without medicine. As a great unexpected bonus, I feel better than ever too.

Through diet, my allergies, athsma, heartburn, rosacea, eczema, and aches and pains are GONE, and we both couldn't be more thankful. I mentioned earlier that my husband, Bob, wouldn't budge on changing his own diet and surely thought I had lost my mind. But one day he came down with "Trigger Finger," and was really scared. I told him to get off sugar. He reluctantly did, but guess what happened...it went away. Even then, he was impressed, but still not swayed.

It was about 5 years later that he tried to donate blood, but the Red Cross wouldn't take his blood because his blood pressure was too high. Yay for them. He was pretty shaken and suddenly got religious about eating right and amping up the exercise. He began to feel better than ever, and was able to not only bring his blood pressure down to normal, without medications. but he also lost 35 pounds, AND is now a believer. Yay Bob! :)

My mom struggled with osteoarthritis, high blood pressure, diabetes, and finally turned to healthy eating. She has dropped 18 pounds and feels better than she has in years.

My dad, at 84 years old, is healthy and active, but changed his diet to support my mom. He feels better than he did, and has lost 12 pounds, without even trying.

My sister, Kristi, joined the bandwagon and has lost over 25 pounds, has greater energy, and looks and feels fantastic.

My sister Pam is eating more healthy and feeling better and her husband Frank, has lost about 20 pounds and feels great. Now it's even spilling over to nieces, nephews and many extended family members. Especially as they realize they can still have amazing food, but feel better while eating it. It's thrilling to see that zest for life return in each of their countenances, as they grasp these changes. One by one we are becoming a very healthy family and it's exciting!

I'm so proud of each one of them, they are my hero's, and it's so rewarding to see each of them feeling better!

www.naturesknockout.com

Your health is the greatest gift you've been given!

PHOTO: JEFFERY HOLT

Laurie Vukich & daughter (and inspiration) Tiffany Correa

So whether you're in this alone or not, it really doesn't matter because you're about to embark on the most amazing reformation of your life, which leaves people feeling vibrant! Because of that, this new way of life is extremely contagious and before you know it the rest of your world will begin climbing on board as well. It's inevitable, because deep down, they know too, that there's nothing better than feeling great.

The pessimist sees the difficulty in every opportunity, the optimist sees the opportunity in every difficulty

—Annonomous

OUR JOURNEY TO FREEDOM

If this isn't passion, we don't know what is. We can hardly wait to get this book to print!

This book, (STEP 2 of our Program) is about "beauty" at its best, intended to help your health soar to a whole new level. Beyond that, we believe this will be the last diet you'll ever need. Did I say "ever"? YES, ever!

STEP 1, was our book "Beauty Bite Desserts" intended to get you off sugar painlessly. We've heard from many of you, who are now OFF sugar, and we're so thrilled and get goose bumps as we hear your stories! Keep up the great work.

The intent of this book is to rebuild from the inside, by amping up the nutrients in your diet, help you to absorb them better, and to boost the body through adding probiotics.

Are you ready for the best "feel good" changes in your life? Welcome to a diet you will never want to give up. We call it a "Pure Foods Diet." We found a great deal of positive research on, and even lived on the "Mediterranean" and the "Raw" diets for years, so this diet is a merge somewhere in between the two.

Our goal is to replace the toxins in our diet with an abundance of nutrients, which can boost the immune system.

12 www.naturesknockout.com

*Enjoy the little things, for one day you may
look back and realize they were the big things
— Robert Brault*

To increase nutrients, we strive for rich, natural color in every meal. The more colorful the vegetable or fruit, the more nutrients you'll usually find. They also add great fiber, which is important too. Food that is easy to digest moves through the system faster and easier, which otherwise could cause inflammation and other disease, and cause the body to age at a faster rate.

Here's a simple way to explain why the digestive system should be moving well: E-choli is poison, right? That's also the very thing that builds up in our systems when our bodies are slow to process what we eat. So in order to feel better, we really need to eat foods that allow our bodies to function as they were meant to. Foods that are processed and not in their natural state are basically cloggers, okay, new word, but get the point?

They slow down the digestive tract and are more likely to back us up, which could cause the body to become "toxic." So, we eat very little of them, if any at all.

Are we vegan? No, not quite, but close. We don't eat any dairy at all, to avoid heartburn and symptoms of lactose intolerance, and arthritis. We do eat occasional meats, which only include hormone and anti-biotic free poultry and fish. Our favorite fish is wild salmon, because of the rich omega3 fatty acids, but other fish we feel are safe to eat include sardines, herring, and black cod or butterfish.

Since our concern is for nutrients, those wild fish are high in omega 3 fatty acids, and protein. We've found Tiffany's body responds favorably when she eliminates meats, however, we feel truly natural meats can offer nutritional benefits and also supply vitamin B12, which the body needs.

Next on the list is eggs, which are very rich in nutrients and B and D vitamins. Because of that, we do eat locally farmed

13

hormone and antibiotic free eggs, here and there.

We're leery of meats marked "natural" that don't say wild or hormone and anti-biotic free, especially since those are big marketing words. If you think about it, any animal could be considered "natural," no matter what it's been pumped full of.

A greater concern with meats is that most commercially raised animals are fed Genetically Modified (GMO) diets. If they are what they eat, we could be in big trouble, too.

We encourage you to read up on GMO's. We stay clear of them completely, and have heard from many viewers who see health improvements after getting away from them. Many countries currently ban them or are in the process, unfortunately that isn't the case in the USA and because of that, the best defense we have is education.

If you want to make your dreams come true, the first thing you have to do is wake up. – J.M. Power

We also avoid anything that is processed or refined. Sugar can be one of the toughest to replace, but based on our own experience and the experience of many of our viewers, we believe that going off sugar alone can make a world of difference (especially in the US, where most of our "sugar" is GMO.

We know some grains shipped from the US have been found to be GMO. So unless it says GMO free, or USDA Certified Organic, we don't take a chance-there are still great replacements. GMO's can also be found in many commercially grown crops, which we've listed on page 23.

We also carefully pick restaurants when we eat out. We really believe our books can change your world and at the very least, you'll walk away realizing that eating healthy can be delicious, and super quick and easy. Our goal was to take every one of our indulgences and replace them with healthy and beauty preserving alternatives.

We can't wait for you to start trying out the recipes and to hear your results. Your skin, physique, hair & nails will love them, but we also believe that you are about to embark on the most overwhelming satisfaction of your life!

What lies behind us and what lies before us are tiny matters compared to what lies within us.
— Henry Stanley Kaskins

www.naturesknockout.com

We realized 3 ways to eliminate potentially dangerous "toxins" from our lives. We could REPLACE the...

PRODUCTS WE USE
THOUGHTS WE THINK
FOODS WE EAT

How toxic foods age us:

We believe many of the foods we eat are toxic to our systems, and that as our bodies reject or fail to process them, inflammation and intolerance sets in, allowing premature aging and disease to take place.

Hormones/antibiotics: Added hormones can throw off our natural balance, causing toxicity. Antibiotics in excess can cause antibiotic resistance & lower our immune system.

GMO's-foods that are genetically modified appear to be heavily laden with toxic chemicals which can lower our immune system.

How toxic beauty products can age us:

Inflammation and other disease can be triggered by potentially "toxic" ingredients that absorb into the bloodstream as they are absorbed.

Endocrine Disruptors. Many "toxic" ingredients work by mimicking estrogen in the system. Too much estrogen can be dangerous, even deadly, and has been linked to reproductive organ cancers, early onset puberty, infertility, and more.

Chemicals that are delivered to our major organs can cause neurotoxicity, cancers, kidney disfunction and more, and should be avoided.

How toxic thoughts can age us:

Stress 1 year = 6 years aging. When our bodies are stressed, cortisol is released into the system which works to destroy healthy cells.

Toxic thoughts work as poison throughout our systems, causing inflammation, disease, lack of sleep, loss of appetite and severe depression, which also causes the body to age much faster.

If we think we are a victim, we let go of hope and a zest for life. As despair sets in, our immune system struggles, causing our health to decline and allowing the body to break down at an accelerated rate.

THE LAST DIET EVER

"The key to change...is to let go of fear."
~ Rosanne Cash

NO NEED FOR FEAR.

Fear is the biggest barrier to most of the change that we know we need to make. But staying locked in fear, keeps us hostage to something much less. As you embrace our strategies, and keep focused on *feeling great,* a smile is bound to fill your face and before you know it, the rest will fall into place.

www.naturesknockout.com

12 STEPS TO SUCCESS

1. REPLACE! Clean out your cupboards right away, and re-stock with foods listed in our pantries in both books. Don't cold turkey off of what you love, just find awesome replacements and you won't be giving up a thing.

2. GET OFF SUGAR PAINLESSLY. if you're not there, make up some of the specialty ice creams in this book, head to our website, or open our Desserts Cookbook. Pick a recipe or two to whip up and have on hand. Just make sure you have some sort of natural sweet substitute every day. Before you know it, the cravings will be gone and you will love that new feeling of empowerment.

3. HAVE 1 GREEN SMOOTHIE EVERY DAY. This step will help tremendously to power load the body with nutrients. And, btw, it will also help curb your craving for sweets. Double whammy.

4. DON'T LET YOURSELF GET HUNGRY. Once you are in hunger mode, all bets are off and the diet suffers. Meal Plan, and add healthy snacks between every meal. Make sure each smoothie, snack, or meal contains a combination of healthy fats, protein, and complex carbs. Also, always leave the house with a snack pack of food.

5. DRINK PLENTY OF WATER. Drink half of your body weight in ounces every day. Make sure to use pure, filtered, or fresh spring water. Get away from thin plastic bottles if you can, as flexible plastic contains BPA and/or BPS, which have been shown to be endocrine disruptors and carcinogenic, especially if exposed to heat.

6. COUNT NUTRIENTS, NOT CALORIES. With our diet, we were so consumed with getting healthy that nutrients were highly coveted. We stopped worrying about calories and the pounds fell off. You'll also notice we don't include nutrition facts, because a 1200 calorie salad will treat the body differently than a 1200 calorie burger. Nutrition facts are also needed for pre-packaged foods, but not for real whole foods.

7. ENJOY FOOD. Sit down to eat without distractions. How often do we scarf down food while sidetracked? If we don't eat: in the car, while watching TV, at the computer, etc., we will naturally begin to enjoy our food more. Also, chewing our food more, as we'll discuss further in this book, will also slow down our digestion and help us enjoy the taste of our food much more.

8. KEEP A JOURNAL. We actually found that after we stopped worrying about calories, the pounds fell off. We also believe in taking a positive approach and making this experience wonderful. I know journaling sounds like work, but doing it for just 1 month (or even 1 week) will help to reprogram the mind. But instead of logging all of your food intake, simply write a few thoughts about all of the good additions you made and how you feel about doing so. That's it. Give yourself stars, smilies, or hearts for your victories. If you fall short, jot down better goals for tomorrow. Also, if you write down your feelings just before you ate "poison" you'll start to recognize your triggers. Once you pinpoint those triggers, you'll notice they begin to lose their power and you won't fall for them again. As that happens, write notes in your journal about how amazing you feel for overcoming!

9. STOP EATING 3 HOURS BEFORE BEDTIME. This will help balance the hormones as it keeps off the fat.

10. MIND GAMES THAT WORK. Use smaller plates. Another good habit to form is to leave something on your plate at the end of every meal. Be positive, stay focused on feeling better. Love life, and love the journey. Also de-stress, by taking time to sleep, breathe deeply, forgive freely, be grateful for each day, and to love more.

11. EXERCISE!! This is the foundation of our diet. If you already exercise every day, keep it up. If not, add 12 minutes of exercise every day for 1 month and don't allow yourself to do more. The reason is: we want you hooked! Then you'll successfully reward yourself with more exercise. Let yourself get to that point, it's amazing!

12.BODY LOVE. Learning to be truly grateful for your body, no matter what state it is in, is essential. Tiffany went through the phase of hating her body for being sick, (which is normal) but in that state, the body struggles even harder to survive. You have a wonderful body that will take care of you, if you treat it right. How incredibly amazing is that?! Once Tiffany realized her body wasn't the enemy, she wanted to care for it again, and consequently began to feel better. She has since said that she is grateful for her disease, which forces her to take care of her body. You have that same wonderful gift, when you see it as that, the victim cycle can end, and healing and empowerment can begin.

soda pop replacement example

Just look at the ingredients in a can of pop. Are there any non-chemical ingredients at all? Studies have shown that not only is that pop void of nutrients, but those chemicals also may deplete your body of vital nutrients it needs to maintain strong bones and overall health. Other issues that have been linked to soda pop include diabetes and heart problems. Ironically diet pop has been associated with weight gain. Here's a cool way to wean away from pop.

COMBINE Organic apple juice or tart cherry juice (great for bedtime, btw) and sparkling water make a great replacement for any soda pop cravings.

shopping list - your new pantry...

The beauty of this book is that the recipes are so easy! When we first started transforming our diets, we avoided books that made us use weird ingredients. But then we slowly started trying things one at a time. Before long we wondered how we'd ever cooked without these wonderful new items. So please look at this list with an open mind and before you know it -- you'll want to make them staples in your pantry too.

This list will help make the transition easy. Everything listed can be used in several recipes in this book. You can find most of these items at a health food store.

FOODS WITH EXCEPTIONALLY HIGH NUTRITIONAL VALUE

* ANTI-INFLAMMATORY BONUS

+ SUPER FOOD
° NATURAL SPF

SPICES & HERBS
- Chives
  Cilantro
- Cinnamon
- Ginger Root
- Mint
  Nutmeg
- Rosemary

HEALTHY FATS:
- Avocados
  Coconut Oil - extra virgin
- EVOO - Extra virgin olive oil
- Flaxseed Oil

UN-ROASTED SEEDS, NUTS & BUTTERS (w/out salt):
- Almond Butter
- Almond pulp (from almond milk recipe)
- Almonds
- Brazil Nuts
- Cashews
- Cashew Butter
- Chia Seeds
- Filberts
- Flax Seeds
- Hazel Nuts
- Macadamia
- Pecans
  Pumpkin Seeds
  Quinoa
  Sesame Seeds
  Sunflower Seeds
  Sun-butter
  Tahini
- +Walnuts

SWEETENERS:
Liquid Stevia
°Dehydrated Stevia Powder (should be green)
Raw Honey
°Dates
°Date Sugar (can be substituted with dates)
Coconut Sugar
Lucuma Powder
Monk Fruit (Lo Han Guo)

FRUITS:
- •+ Acai
- • Areolas
- •+°Goji Berries
- • Apples
  Bananas
- •+°Blueberries
- • Cantaloupe
  Coconut
  Dates
  Grapes
- • Guavas
  Kiwi
  Lemons
  Limes
- •° Lincoln Berries
- • Olives
- • Melons
  Mangos
  Oranges
- • Papayas
- • Peaches
- • Pineapple
  Raisins
- +° Raspberries
- • Strawberries
  °Watermelon

VEGETABLES:
- °Beets
- °Beet Greens
- °Bell Peppers
- •°Carrots
  Celery
- • Collards
  °Dandelion Greens
  °Dark Field Greens
- • °Grape Leaves
- •+°Kale
- • °Kelp
- • Mushrooms (Shiitake)
- • Onions
- • °Peppers (jalapeño)
- • °Pumpkin
  °Romaine Lettuce
- • °Spinach
- •° Sweet Potatoes
  Tomatillos
  °Tomatoes

NUTRIENTS & FLAVOR:
- •+Cacao Powder
- •+Cacao Nibs
  Vanilla Extract
  Acidophilus
- +Maca
  Nutritional Yeast
  Probiotic Powder
  Kiefer granules or live culture starter

VEGAN DAIRY:
Almond Milk
Coconut Milk
Coconut Milk Kiefer
Coconut Milk Yogurt
Rice Milk

THINK SMART

A successful man can lay a firm foundation with the bricks others throw at him.

— Sidney Greenberg

what to buy organic

To make it simple, most produce that has a thick peel, we don't buy organic. But others can have high levels of pesticide and should be purchased organic. Here's our list, based on the EWG's annual Dirty Dozen List for fruits & vegetables...

FRUIT TO BUY ORGANIC.
Apples
Strawberries & Blueberries
Peaches & Nectarines

GRAINS. BUY ALL ORGANIC, if used at all.

VEGETABLES TO BUY ORGANIC.
4 greens: Celery, Spinach Lettuce & Kale
Bell peppers,
Potatoes

what about USDA certified organic?

In the US, in order to receive USDA Certified Organic labeling, a products can't contain GMO's. Here are GMO crops to avoid...

Alfalfa	Cottonseed (oil)	Sugar
Canola	Zucchini	Soy
Corn	Summer Squash	Papaya

what to keep an eye on

Foods currently awaiting FDA approval as GMO's include Salmon, Granny Smith & Golden Delicious apples. Also watch ingredients in vitamins, which are derived from GMO corn: ascorbic (Vit C), amino, lactic and citric acids, tocopherals (Vit E), yeast, molasses, artificial & natural flavorings, aspartame, sucrose, xanthan gum

www.naturesknockout.com

a dehydrator?!!

You don't have to have a dehydrator to cook the way that we cook, but we've found it to be a wonderful asset. In fact, we keep our dehydrators running all the time, whether it's to dry soaked nuts, make yogurts, dry greens for smoothies, and more.

One thing we've found that saves us a fortune is that as soon as fruits or veggies are on the verge of getting too ripe, we cut them up and let them dry out. That way we don't waste anything and have a good supply of food we can reconstitute very quickly, or add to stews or smoothies.

If you don't want to invest a lot, less expensive dehydrators can be used. I started with a $30 one and have moved up to a $200 one, which works out a lot better for me.

green smoothies on the road

In our travels, we find it really difficult to make green smoothies. Here's a great little tip that helps get the benefits, flavor, and nutrients on the go. When we make green smoothies at home, we make them extra big, and then place a non-stick sheet in our dehydrator. We smooth on coconut oil and pour out the green smoothie. We let it run overnight for a wonderful treat anytime!

24

SWEET THINGS

"An obstacle is often a stepping stone." – Prescott

raw sweeteners

The following are great raw sweeteners, although not all of them are used in this book. Please refer to

YAKON SYRUP. A superfood, low-glycemic sweetener, caramel or maple flavor - use in place of agave

LACUMA. A caramel flavored sweetener rich in nutrients, from Peru.

DATES, DATE SUGAR. Nutrient rich fruit that is dehydrated then granulated. Make sure to pit them before using (I learned this the hard way, literally! :)

RAISINS. Great in cereals, smoothies and more. The darker the color, the richer in nutrients!

RAW HONEY. Use 3/4 cup honey to substitute 1 cup of sweetener. Tiffany can't have regular honey, but raw honey hasn't been heat processed and works great for her. Local raw honey is best for boosting immunities.

BANANAS. Never throw a banana away! In smoothies, the blacker, the better!

MONK FRUIT. A natural herbal sweetener with medicinal properties. 300x the strength of sugar and in it's pure form, should be a brown color. Avoid any form of this that is trademarked.

RAW STEVIA/STEVIA DROPS. A very nutritious green herb--IMPORTANT: make sure it isn't white or a trademarked brand. Company's can't trademark a natural substance, so they change it chemically and call it a similar name. We prefer stevia only in green powder form, or drops that are simply just stevia extract. Stevia is great as a sugar substitute, but bulk must be added.

Do not let what you cannot do interfere with what you can do. – John Wooden

NOT SO SWEET SWEETENERS

"NATURAL" SWEETENERS WE DON'T USE IN THIS BOOK: PROCESSED SWEETENERS. Barley Malt Syrup, Brown Rice, Syrup, Maple Syrup, Coconut Sugar
These sweeteners are considered natural, but are heat processed, so if we use them, it is in baked goods, that will be heated anyway. For that reason, you won't find any of them in this book.

"NATURAL" SWEETENERS WE AVOID. Agave Nectar, Cane Sugar, Sucanat, Corn Sugar, Brown Sugar, White Sugar, White Stevia, Fructose, Molasses, Xylitol

We tried several of these sugars, but Tiffany had a great deal of inflammation each time for several days afterward. That of course, led us to more research, where we learned that each of these sweeteners are heat processed, and that is what we believe is the problem. Our guess is that the high temperature processing alters the chemical construction causing it to act as a foreign invader to some, especially those who may be chemical intolerant.

www.naturesknockout.com

a bit of honey

RAW HONEY FOR HEALTH.

Honey has been used for centuries for it's medicinal and healing properties. It has been touted for it's anti-bacterial, anti-viral and anti-fungal qualities, yet at the same time is very rich in antioxidants and friendly bacteria.

Other phytonutrients found in honey have been linked to the inhibition of cancers and may promote optimal glucose metabolism. It is also touted as an immunity booster which can aid in the healing of ulcers, burns and wounds, with the ability to increase athletic performance.

When heated, many of the healing properties of honey can be lost, so the honey is no longer considered "raw." In Tiffany's case, we've found she can eat raw honey, but processed honey causes inflammation and must be avoided.

A spoonful of raw honey can help alleviate a cough (although should not be given to children 1 year old or younger.) Two spoonfuls a day can help boost the Immune System and relieve allergies and hay fever as well. For best results local "raw"honey is most effective.

Raw honey is really delicious in any of the cacao (chocolate) flavored smoothies, especially when it is thick because it takes on a yummy caramel flavor--mmm.

27

DRINK UP

The foolish man seeks happiness in the distance; the wise man grows it under his feet. ~ James Openheim

hydrate for beauty

Our bodies were mostly water at one time, but as we age, the water reserves begin to appear to dry out. Drinking enough water is essential, as we discussed earlier, but the real secret is to also add more healthy oils, fruits and vegetables to our daily diets as well, for a healthy youthful glow. So, to beautify the skin, we enjoy more smoothies, and always add healthy fats and balance them with healthy proteins for a complete snack or meal.

nut milks

Delicious, simple to make, and another great way to add protein to your smoothie.

green smoothies

Green smoothies provide great way to get 8-12 or more fresh fruits and vegetables in your diet every day. It's also great to add some wonderful nutrients by adding probiotics, goji berries, nuts, seeds, flax seed, spices, protein, etc. One thing to remember is the importance of chewing food along with a smoothie (or drinking them slowly and waiting to swallow,) in order to benefit more from your natural digestive enzymes.

teas

Herbal & Spice teas can be very beneficial, therapeutic and refreshing, but we try not to overheat water for teas. In order to maintain the integrity of the beverage, we only use warmed waters.

The best way to cheer yourself up is to cheer somebody else up ~Mark Twain

face-lift frappe

This drink is one of our favorite anti-aging secrets. We feel it works well for skin that is dry, wrinkled, saggy and needs a lift, or just to look and feel younger. We've also noticed skin with breakouts of acne, rosacea, and eczema turn around beautifully, as well. We drink this delicious frappe every day if we can!

1 cup organic apple juice
2 ounces *aloe vera juice
2 tablespoons hormone free gelatin (optional)
1 tablespoon chia seeds
1 tablespoon extra virgin olive oil
1 tablespoon lemon juice
1 teaspoon acidophilus

Shake or whip all ingredients up in a little personal blender for a frothy treat, or if you don't have a lot of time, just stir it up and go.

beauty bonus

ANTI-AGING TONER
We love this drink to tone and hydrate the skin externally as well. Reserve 1 tablespoon of it, then apply to face and neck with a clean cotton ball just after cleansing.

Many of life's failures are experienced by people who did not realize how close they were to success when they gave up – Thomas Edison

beauty tidbits

Understanding the skin and what makes it flourish can make a world of difference in preserving and nourishing it. Here are some of beauty's best friends…

Moisture is the key to preserving the skin. Since water alone can't do it, each of these ingredients are wonderful hydrators. When used in conjunction with one another they provide a super hydration inside and out.

•**gelatin** has been shown to repair tissues and organs and is a major component of cell membranes. As it builds strong, watertight membranes, it fully hydrates, reducing the appearance of wrinkles and reduces signs of aging.

•**Olive oil and flaxseed**, which are loaded with Omega 3 fatty acids work wonders for the body, skin, nails and hair. They are also beneficial in protecting the skin from the sun too.

•**Lemon** is considered in holistic medicine as a detoxifier, which the liver and skin both can respond well to.

•**Apples** are loaded with anti-oxidants and contain immune system boosting quercetin, which makes me think they can "help keep the doctor away." Very replenishing and nourishing and also anti-aging, and can do wonders for your skin as well. Apples are often used as natural "stem cell" ingredients in skin care, for that reason.

•**Aloe Vera juice** (not recommended if you're pregnant or nursing) has an ongoing list of ways it can benefit the body, but also has been linked to aiding in cellular repair, leaving the skin appearing younger as it super-hydrates the skin.

Do not go where the path may lead; go instead where there is no path and leave a trail.— anonymous

rice milk

1 cup soaked brown rice
4-5 cups filtered water
1 vanilla bean (optional)
1/4 teaspoon liquid stevia (optional)

Place ingredients in blender and mix 2-3 minutes. If more sweetness is desired add the inside of the vanilla bean and stevia. Strain with a nut milk bag into a pitcher and serve. Keeps up to 5 days refrigerated.

almond milk

1 cup soaked almonds
4-5 cups filtered water
1 vanilla bean (optional)
1/4 teaspoon liquid stevia (optional)

Place ingredients in blender and mix 2-3 minutes. If more sweetness is desired add the inside of the vanilla bean and stevia. Strain with a nut milk bag into a pitcher and serve. Keeps up to 5 days refrigerated.

almond beauty

Almonds have been found to be good for the skin, heart, cardio, blood sugar and for boosting the immune system.

smart tip
Eating a handful of almonds a day has been shown to increase brain capacity and clarity.

www.naturesknockout.com

coconut milk

1 cup unsweetened coconut flakes
2 cups filtered or spring water
1 vanilla bean (optional)
1/2 teaspoon liquid stevia (optional)

Pour coconut flakes into a high quality blender, and blend until powdery. Then add water and mix well for 2-3 minutes. Strain with cheesecloth or a nut milk bag. Pour milk into pitcher, or if more sweetness is desired add the inside of the vanilla bean and stevia.

coconut cream

This is delicious on desserts, pancakes, french toast, in smoothies and in warm teas or cereals. It instantly turns any dish into a savory treat! Keeps 2-3 weeks refrigerated.

1/2 cup raw cashews
2/3 cup shredded coconut
1/3 cup coconut milk
1 teaspoon liquid stevia
1/2 tablespoon pure vanilla
pinch of sea salt

Place all ingredients in blender and blend well Refrigerate 1 hour before serving. Store in refrigerator.

for beauty...

Coconuts contain lauric acid, which is naturally found in mother's milk and helps build the immune system as it kills viruses, bacteria, parasites, fungi, and yeast. Also full of nutrients including calcium, magnesium and amino acids. Coconut milk, water, and butter are very moisturizing and nourishing to the hair and skin, whether applied topically or ingested.

sports drink...

Coconut water is a wonderful natural drink which hydrates at the same time. It has been shown to be beneficial to the digestive system as it detoxifies and cleanses. By carrying oxygen to the cells, it can help increase circulation. Rich in nutrients, also shown to be anti-viral, anti-microbial, and anti-fungal. It naturally contains 20% potassium and no chemicals. Compare that to commercial sports drinks, with 1% potassium and a lot of chemicals.

why yogurt & kefir?!

Yogurt is another incredible beauty food. It is typically FULL of probiotics, which are one of nature's little blessings in our lives. They help the digestive system by replenishing "friendly" bacteria, which allows healing within the body at the ultimate source. Translated, that means more beautiful, glowing skin, as well. In fact, when fighting skin disorders, eczema, and dermatitis; probiotics are a great addition to the diet, and are even more effective when added 3x per day.

But if you browse through grocery store yogurt, you are likely to see a lot of chemicals, sugars, artificial colors, and flavors. We question the good that is left in those products and feel much better making our own, which is simple to do.

Oh, and ps. you don't even need a yogurt maker for these recipes!

Health is the greatest possession. Contentment is the greatest treasure. Confidence is the greatest friend.
Lao Tzu

magic yogurt

We call this "magic" yogurt, because it's so simple to make and because of the amazing health and beauty benefits it offers.

- 1/3 cup plain, raw, or organic yogurt with live cultures or a package of coconut milk kefir grains (purchase at a health food store or online) or 4 capsules of pure probiotic powder (remove the capsules before using!)
- 4 cups organic coconut milk (allow to set so the cream settles on top. Use only the cream for thicker yogurt (the rest can be used in ice cream or a smoothie)
- 2 tablespoons organic unflavored gelatin or tapioca starch, or 2 teaspoons guar gum
- 1 teaspoon pure stevia extract (optional)
- 1 teaspoon pure vanilla extract (optional)

Stir the yogurt (starter) and coconut milk together in a glass bowl. If you want to add the flavors now, you can, but if you want tart yogurt for sour creams, etc, you should add them later.

Cover with a damp cotton rag and place in a dehydrator (if you have one that is a box type) or, you could place it in a dark area on a heat pad (on the lowest setting), or even in an oven with only the light on. The temperature shouldn't be higher than 110° in whichever "incubator" you choose.

•Coconut milk should set 24 hours. It won't thicken as much as dairy, but will still be great and loaded with nutritional value! (If you are using organic or raw cow or goat's milk, it should be ready in 7-8 hours)

Remove from heat source. Stir and cover, and place in the refrigerator for 3-4 hours. Done!

quick kefir

Make a batch of plain, magic yogurt. For kefir, you can use 3 cans full cream coconut milk and won't need to separate out just the cream.

To serve: pour 1 1/2 cups yogurt into a mini blender. Add:

• 2 squirts liquid stevia extract

• 1/2 teaspoon pure vanilla extract

Blend together and serve as it is, or add in fresh fruit of your choice and mix. That's it!

instant whey

Whey is the juice that settles on the top of yogurt. Don't get grossed out, just scoop it off and make super nutritious probiotic juices!

cream cheese

I actually made this by accident after I removed the whey from some yogurt and forgot about the yogurt. Over a month, it thickened up nicely into a wonderful cream cheese! And I thought making cheese was supposed to be hard. :)

35

PROBIOTIC JUICES

It's not whether you get knocked down, it's whether you get up. – Vince Lombardi

The power of probiotics in the body and the healing benefits they provide, are astounding! What makes these beautiful for the body is that the live active cultures in these drinks begin a fermentation process, which will make them slightly bubbly (in fact, be ready for the gases to pop a bit when you first open the containers), but the nutritional content is astounding in the early stages of fermentation.

But unlike their alcoholic counterparts, at this stage, these juices don't contain dangerous levels of alcohol. We do not recommend consuming alcohol, which dehydrates the brain, skin, and serves as a vicious enemy to our vital organs.

www.naturesknockout.com

What the mind of man can conceive and believe, it can achieve. – Friedrich Nietzsche

ginger ale

This is our favorite probiotic juice, it tastes great, and the lemon in it can be cleansing, while the ginger provides immediate anti-inflammatory benefits, making it a delicious BEAUTY drink, as well--AND all of these juices are wonderful in any of our smoothies, or shakes!

- 1/3 - 1/2 cup fresh lemon juice
- 2/3 cup raw honey
- 2" chunk of fresh ginger
- 1/4 cup whey (juice separated from your yogurt)
- 1 teaspoon cinnamon
- 2 quarts filtered water
- dash of sea salt
-

Directions are on the bottom of page 38...

Whether you think you can or think you can't,
you're right – Henry Ford

lemon twist

- Juice from 5 lemons
- Juice from 2 limes
- 1/2 cup raw honey + green stevia powder (to taste)
- 1/2 cup whey (juice separated from your yogurt)
- 1/8 teaspoon sea salt
- 1/2 teaspoon cinnamon
- 1 quart filtered water

lime delight

- Juice from 8 limes
- 1/2 cup raw honey + green stevia powder (to taste)
- 1/2 cup whey (juice separated from your yogurt)
- 1/4 teaspoon sea salt
- 1/4 teaspoon cinnamon
- 1 1/2 quarts filtered water

pineapple splash

- Juice from 1 large pineapple
- 1/2 cup honey
- 1/2 cup whey (juice separated from your yogurt)
- juice from 1 lemon (2 Tablespoons)
- 1/4 teaspoon sea salt
- 1 1/2 quarts filtered water

DIRECTIONS FOR EACH OF THESE RECIPES. Mix all ingredients except water together in a blender, then add in the water and pour into a large glass container. Place a lid on it and allow to sit in a dark area for 2-6 days. You can burp the lid 1x per day, to relieve the pressure.

After 2 days, you can keep it in the refrigerator. It will continue to taste better each day that it sits.

HOW TO MAKE A PERFECT SMOOTHIE

always include these items...

1. **complex carbs** - fresh veggies & fruits
2. **protein** - nuts, seeds, cultured yogurt
3. **healthy fats** - extra virgin olive oil, flaxseed oil, avocado, coconut oil
4. bonus--probiotics

NOTE: Some of the smoothies and shakes in this book provide all of the above items. If they don't, we enjoy them with a meal or snack to make sure every meal is complete with each of these four items.

PROTEIN.

It's great to add protein to the smoothie to balance it out and fill you up. If you use a protein powder, just make sure the ingredients are real food items. Another great protein to add is chia seeds (1-2 tablespoons)

I often will omit the protein from the smoothie, and instead opt to eat nuts, seeds, or a homemade trail mix or nut bar along with the smoothie, in order to maximize the benefit.

HEALTHY FATS.

Our favorites--avocado, flaxseed oil, extra virgin olive oil, walnut oil, or last, but not least, coconut oil!

PROBIOTICS.

These are essential for healing the gut and great for those with skin issues. Find them in our yogurt, kefir, or our probiotic juices.

LIQUID & SWEETENER.

Add water, nut, rice, or coconut milk, or probiotic juices. Sweeten with fruit, dates, stevia or raw honey. Adding in any of our ice cream, or sherbets work great too. Now blend!

nutrient absorption

If you aren't absorbing the wonderful nutrients you're eating, you won't see the full benefit. Two ways to get better absorption are by: **Adding Healthy Fats**, and **by chewing** nuts, seeds, anything, alongside your smoothie, in order to activate the digestive enzymes which aid in nutrient absorption.

perfect balance

In our quest for a more healthy diet, one thing we found many people have varying opinions on is the ratio of proteins, carbs, and fats in the diet. The one thing they agreed on was the need for balance, just how much is all relative.

So what we've done is focus, not so much on exact ratios, but on the need to have complex carbs, proteins, and healthy fats every time we eat. If we're eating protein from nuts or seeds, we can have less fruit and vegetables than if we are combining them with animal proteins. Since animal proteins are more difficult to digest, more fiber will be necessary to move them through our systems.

The Mediterranean Diet is notorious for having miraculous healing effects on the body, which in part, is attributed to healthy fats, which are rich in omega 3 fatty acids. It doesn't mean we should guzzle olive oil, but instead, simply replace it with all butters and other fats.

If we were to chart out our diet, here are the approximate ratios we would shoot for:

45--55% **Complex carbs**, 25-35% **protein**, 20-30% **fat**

We just add what is missing each time we eat, so we can maintain that important balance. Also note that we avoid ALL simple carbs in our diets.

Many people shy away from the fats, but we say stay away from the trans-fatty acids and most of the saturated fats altogether. They will tend to age the body faster. So when it comes to the fats in the diet, we feel the more healthy fats (listed on page 39) in your day, the more beautiful your skin, nails and hair will appear as well.

*It wasn't raining when Noah built an ark –
Howard Ruff*

GREEN SMOOTHIE HEROES

We've found that the more vegetables we add to our smoothies, the more detoxifying they can be. When we need a boost and more energy and mental clarity, we do some of our no or low fruit smoothies. But when the body is healthy, we enjoy adding more fruit, which is loaded in nutrients, especially when purchased in season. The following lists include some of our favorite fruits and vegetables.

greens

Not sure which greens to use? Here are some great options. We feel it is best to change it up and not have the same thing every day.

Cilantro.
Vit. A, C, K, said to absorb toxins, so we only buy organic

Collard Greens.
High antioxidant levels. Vit. A, C, K, folate, manganese & calcium - slightly bitter

Grape Leaves.
Vit. A, C, E, K, B6, niacin, iron, fiber, riboflavin, folate, calcium, magnesium,   copper and manganese - mild with a slightly tart or bitter flavor

Kale.
High antioxidant levels. Vit. A, C, calcium & iron - stronger flavor

Spinach.
Vit. A, B6, C, folate, niacin, calcium - mild flavor. ONLY eat organic. Consumed in excess, raw spinach may cause acne.

Swiss Chard.
A, C, K magnesium, manganese, potassium and iron - salty flavor

Italian Parsley.
Vit. A, C, K, folate, iron & calcium - moderate flavor

Dandelion Greens.
Vit. A, C, E, K, calcium & iron, great detox - used to cleanse kidneys,   liver,   and gallbladder - stronger flavor

Beet Greens.
Vit. A, C & calcium - light flavor

Turnip Greens.
Vit. C & calcium - stronger flavor

41   www.naturesknockout.com

What we dwell on is what we become – Oprah Winfrey

OTHER VEGGIES GOOD IN SHAKES, SMOOTHIES OR JUICES.

SQUASH.
Because some are GMO's, we recommend only buying certified organic
Pumpkin, Zucchini, and Spaghetti Squash are our favorites. They tend to add more bulk, so usually a 1/2 cup is plenty in a 4 cup smoothie.
CUCUMBERS.
CELERY.
CABBAGE.
BEETS.

FRUITS.
Use whatever is in season, ratio is about 25% fruits to greens, yummy fresh or frozen. If fresh, add ice to the smoothie.

Fruit does add more "sugar" to the recipe, so if you need to watch your sugars, lean toward our smoothies without fruit, and rely on stevia or dates, depending upon your sensitivities.

SMOOTHIES & SHAKES

IMPORTANT TIPS:

CHEW. I'll say this again, since many of you may be page skippers, like me: Ha, busted! :) Make sure to chew along with your smoothie or shake for the most benefit. We'll often eat a handful of nuts for protein, or a whole apple...the important thing is to chew, in order to activate the digestive enzymes. They aid in nutrient absorption, which is what makes these smoothies so beneficial.

Chewing food more in general is vital to help the digestive tract function better. It also helps keep the body more trim, which is a great benefit, but if that's not enough, chewing also helps make foods more enjoyable and even taste better.

My dad always said to chew each bite 35 times...get counting! :)

ROTATE FOODS. When we eat the same foods every day, we can become susceptible to developing food allergies to them. Make sure to try lots of different smoothies and rotate at least every 4 days.

www.naturesknockout.com

Happiness is a way of travel, not a destination
— Roy L. Goodman

pina-berry shake
2 cups greens of choice
1 cup ORANGE SENSATION PROBIOTIC JUICE
or water
1/2 teaspoon stevia powder
1 cup frozen berries (strawberries, blueberries,
raspberries)
1 cup frozen pineapple
2 tablespoons healthy fat
1 handful goji berries
10 cubes of ice

Blend kale, 1/4 c milk & Stevia to purée.

Add berries, pineapple & blend.. Texture should
be thick so slowly add small amounts of water &
blend till desired consistency is that of a shake.

Top with goji berries.

pineapple banana shake
2 cups frozen pineapple
1 frozen banana
1/2 cup frozen grapes
2 cups almond or coconut milk
1/2 teaspoon stevia
1/2 lime
2 tablespoons healthy fat
10 cubes ice

Mix together in blender and serve.

The man who removes a mountain begins by carrying small stones — Chinese Proverb

pina colada
cream smoothie

1 cup frozen pineapple
1 cup MAGIC YOGURT or knifer, or coconut milk
1/2 cup LIME DELIGHT PROBIOTIC JUICE or 1/2 lime
1 banana
2 cups greens of choice
1/4 teaspoon stevia (optional)
2 tablespoons healthy fat
10 cubes ice

Mix together in blender and serve.

Love is a fruit in season at all times, and within reach of every hand – Mother Teresa

orange cream
smoothie

This is the first smoothie recipe I created on my own, but is still one of my favorites. If you love creamy orange pops, this is a perfect replacement! Plus, oranges have been shown to be beneficial for the skin, improve circulation, cholesterol, digestion, heart, fight illness, including cancer and kidney stones.

1 cup coconut or almond milk
1 cup greens of choice
1/4 teaspoon stevia (optional)
2 tablespoons healthy fat
1 cup frozen pineapple (frozen is best)
1 small banana (fresh or frozen)
2 small oranges (peeled)
1 cup fresh pineapple
1 scoop creamy vanilla protein or maca powder (optional)
2 handfuls Ice

In high quality purée rice milk, collard leaves, stevia & flaxseed oil till smooth. Add pineapple, banana & oranges and blend till desired consistency. Add ice for more thick texture. (optional) Makes 4 cups.

46

orange paradise
smoothie

1 cup coconut milk
1/2 cup ORANGE SENSATION PROBIOTIC JUICE or 1
orange, peeled
1 cup frozen pineapple
1/2 cup frozen mango
1 banana
1 fresh lime
1/4 teaspoon stevia
2 tablespoons healthy fat
10 ice cubes

Mix together in blender and serve.

"The wish for healing has always been half of health."
~ Lucius Annaeus Seneca

citrus cream smoothie

1 cup coconut milk
1 cup fresh pineapple
1/2 cup PINEAPPLE SPLASH or additional coconut milk
2 cups greens of choice
1 lime, peeled
1 cup fresh pineapple
2 Tablespoons healthy fat
1 scoop creamy vanilla protein or maca root powder
1/4 teaspoon green stevia powder
8-10 ice cubes
3 Tablespoons MAGIC YOGURT or kefir

Mix together in blender and barely stir in Magic yogurt or kefir.

www.naturesknockout.com

orange mint
smoothie

1 cup coconut milk
1/2 cup PINEAPPLE SPLASH or orange juice
2 cups greens of choice
2 oranges peeled
1 banana
2 Tablespoons healthy fat
1/4 teaspoon green stevia powder
8-10 ice cubes
1 sprig of fresh mint
3 Tablespoons MAGIC YOGURT, or Kefir (optional)

Mix together in blender and barely stir in Magic yogurt,
kefir., or FRENCH VANILLA ICE CREAM. Add 1 more
spoonful of it to the top as well.

key lime pie
cheesecake smoothie

1 cup MAGIC YOGURT, QUICK KEIFER, or nut milk
1 cup LIME DELIGHT PROBIOTIC JUICE, or 2 Tbsp. lime juice
1/2 cup LIME KIWI SHERBET (optional, but yummy!)
1 cup frozen pineapple
1 scoop creamy vanilla protein or maca root powder
2 cups greens of choice
1 lime
2 Tablespoons healthy fat
1/2 teaspoon green stevia powder
8-10 ice cubes
Mix together in blender and serve.

www.naturesknockout.com

Pineapple
lime cheesecake

1 cup coconut milk
1/2 cup MAGIC YOGURT, QUICK KEIFER or nut milk
1 cup frozen pineapple
1 lime, or LIME DELIGHT PROBIOTIC JUICE
1 scoop creamy vanilla or maca protein powder
1/2 cup greens of choice
2 Tablespoons healthy fat
1/4 teaspoon green stevia powder
8-10 ice cubes

Mix together in blender and serve.

mmmm...mango smoothie

1 mango, peeled, pitted & frozen
1 frozen banana
1 peeled orange or ORANGE SENSATION JUICE
1 cup coconut or almond milk
2 Tablespoons healthy fat
8-10 ice cubes
1/2 teaspoon stevia or raw honey to taste
Mix together in blender and serve.

mango pineapple twist

1 cup water
1 cup LIME KIWI SHERBET or 1/2 lime
1 cup frozen mango
1 fresh orange, peeled
1 cup greens of choice
2 Tablespoons healthy fat
1/2 teaspoon green stevia powder
8-10 ice cubes
Mix together in blender and serve.

mango tango

1 cup TANGY LEMONADE, GINGER ALE or water
1 cup mango
1 cup strawberries
1 cup PEACH'S N CREAM SHERBET, or peaches
2 Tablespoons healthy fat
1/2 teaspoon green stevia powder
8-10 ice cubes
Mix together in blender and serve.

fat burner tip

1 whole mango
Eat up!

mango zip
smoothie

1 cup MAGIC YOGURT or coconut milk
1/2 cup TANGY LEMONADE - or juice
from 1 lemon
1 cup mango
1 cup peaches or PEACH'S N CREAM
SHERBET
2 cups greens of choice
2 Tablespoons healthy fat
1/2 teaspoon green stevia powder
8-10 ice cubes

Mix together in blender and serve.

www.naturesknockout.com

mango lime tart
smoothie

1 cup GINGER ALE or water
1 full lime, peeled
1 cup peaches or PEACH'S N CREAM
SHERBET
1/2 cup mango
1/2 cup fresh pineapple
1-2 cups greens of choice
2 Tablespoons healthy fat
1/2 teaspoon green stevia powder
8-10 ice cubes

Mix together in blender and serve.

kiwi lime pie
smoothie

1 cup coconut water or LIME DELIGHT
1 whole kiwi
2 cups greens of choice
1/2 lime, with some peel
1-2 Tablespoons MAGIC YOGURT
1 cup fresh pineapple
1 scoop creamy vanilla protein powder or maca root powder (optional)
2 Tablespoons healthy fat
1/2 teaspoon green stevia powder
8-10 ice cubes

Mix together in blender and serve.

kiwi cream kicker
smoothie

1 cup QUICK KEIFER or coconut milk
1/2 cup LIME KIWI SHERBET or 1/2 lime
2 cups greens of choice
2 cups frozen grapes
1 frozen banana
1" fresh ginger root
1/2 teaspoon ground cinnamon
2 Tablespoons healthy fat
1/2 teaspoon green stevia powder
8-10 ice cubes

Mix until creamy and serve. Top with
FRENCH VANILLA ICE CREAM.

www.naturesknockout.com

Pina-green colada
smoothie

1 cup coconut milk
2 cups fresh pineapple
2 cups greens of choice
1/2 cup PINEAPPLE SPLASH (optional)
2 tablespoons coconut oil
2 tablespoons unsweetened coconut chips
2 Tablespoons MAGIC YOGURT, kefir, or FRENCH VANILLA ICE CREAM
1 teaspoon freshly ground chia seeds
2 Tablespoons healthy fat
1/2 teaspoon green stevia powder
8-10 ice cubes

Mix together in blender and serve.

Improving your health is a way to improve your happiness =)

kiwi quench
1 cup QUICK KEIFER
1 cup LEMON TWIST or 2 Tbsp. lemon juice
2 kiwis
2 cups greens of choice
2 Tablespoons healthy fat
1/2 teaspoon green stevia powder
8-10 ice cubes

Blend. Top with 2 tablespoons pomegranate seeds and serve.

kiwi lime squeeze
1 cup nut milk
1 whole kiwi
1 cup greens of choice
1 cup frozen pineapple
1/2 cup LIME DELIGHT or 1 lime
2 Tablespoons healthy fat
1/2 teaspoon green stevia powder
8-10 ice cubes

Mix together in blender and serve.

lime a la cream
smoothie

1 cup coconut milk
1/2 cup MAGIC YOGURT or FRENCH VANILLA ICE
CREAM (optional)
2 cups greens of choice
1 small banana
1 lime
1/2 fresh avocado
1 cup greens of choice
1/4 teaspoon green stevia powder
5-6 ice cubes

Mix all ingredients in blender until smooth.
www.naturesknockout.com

lime bliss
1 cup water or nut milk
1 fresh lime
2 cups greens of choice
1/2" fresh ginger root
2 Tablespoons healthy fat
1/2 teaspoon green stevia powder
8-10 ice cubes

peach tango
1 cup PEACH'S N CREAM SHERBET or peaches
1/2 cup QUICK KEIFER
1/2 cup LEMON TWIST or juice from 1 lemon
1 banana
1 scoop creamy vanilla protein powder, or maca root powder (optional)
1 cup greens of choice
1/2" fresh ginger root
2 Tablespoons healthy fat
1/4 teaspoon green stevia powder
8-10 ice cubes

BOTH ABOVE: Mix together in blender and serve.

blueberry smoothie
1 cup tart cherry juice
1 cup greens of choice
1 cup frozen blueberries
1 frozen banana
2 Tablespoons healthy fat
1/2 teaspoon green stevia powder
8-10 ice cubes

blue baby smoothie
1 cup coconut milk
1 cup blueberries
1/2 lime
1 tablespoon creamy vanilla protein or maca powder
2 bunches greens of choice
2 Tablespoons healthy fat
1/2 teaspoon green stevia powder
8-10 ice cubes

BOTH RECIPES: Mix together all ingredients, until smooth.

sweet dandy
creamer

Yes, dandelions! They are power loaded with nutrients and can save you some money too! They will be best before the flowers turn to seed, when they are less bitter.

1 cup coconut milk
1/2 cup MAGIC YOGURT, KEFIR or FRENCH VANILLA ICE CREAM
1 handful dandelion or any other greens
1/2 lime with some skin
2 tablespoons extra virgin olive oil
1 cup blueberries
1 scoop vanilla protein powder or maca root powder
1 /2 teaspoon stevia or other sweetener of choice
a few ice cubes
Blend together and serve. If you like a thinner consistency, add 1 more cup of water and more honey to taste.

berry pink smoothie

1 cup QUICK KEIFER, MAGIC YOGURT, or coconut milk
1/2 cup LIME DELIGHT (or 2 Tbsp. lime juice)
1 cup frozen berries
1/4 slice of raw beet
1-2 cups greens of choice
2 Tablespoons healthy fat
1/2 teaspoon green stevia powder
8-10 ice cubes

sleepytime smoothie

1 cup LEMON or LIME PROBIOTIC JUICE
1 cup frozen berries
1/4 slice of raw beet
1 scoop creamy vanilla protein or maca powder
2 tablespoons Tart Cherry Juice
1-2 cups greens of choice
6 ice cubes
2 tablespoons healthy fat
1 /2 teaspoon stevia

BOTH RECIPES: Mix together in blender and serve. Top with FRENCH VANILLA ICE CREAM (optional).

coconut berry
cream smoothie

This was one of the first delicious smoothies Tiffany came up with. She called me, so excited to share it and I loved that she did. It soon became a favorite for me too!

3/4 cup QUICK KEIFER or MAGIC YOGURT, or FRENCH VANILLA ICE CREAM
1/2 cup filtered water or PINEAPPLE SPLASH
1 1/2 cups greens of choice
2 tablespoons coconut oil
2 cups frozen strawberries, blackberries, blueberries or raspberries
1/2 teaspoon green stevia powder
1-2 handfuls of ice cubes

Blend kefir, water and spinach together until smooth. Add oil and berries and mix until smooth.

64   www.naturesknockout.com

cacao banana split
cream smoothie

This delicious shake came about when my friend, Carlie, was pregnant and craving chocolate. She was worried about giving her baby the best nutrients and asked for a recipe. After a little playing in the kitchen, this yummy treat evolved. Thank you Carlie!

1 frozen banana
1 cup almond or coconut milk
2 tablespoons raw honey or sweetener of choice
1 teaspoon vanilla extract
2-3 tablespoons cacao (or carob) powder
1 tablespoon coconut oil, flaxseed oil, or extra virgin olive oil
1 cup fresh greens
5 ice cubes
Sprinkle with raw cacao nibs

Blend ingredients together, except walnuts. Add nuts and pulse. Makes 2 servings.

65

chocolate-butter
cream smoothie

This is a wonderful quick smoothie. Usually I love to add ice, but not to this one, because it keeps a rich, creamy texture and adds to the great flavor.

MAKES 2 CUPS
1 cup coconut milk
3 tablespoons raw cacao (or carob) powder
2 tablespoons sun-butter
1/2" fresh ginger (or cinnamon)
1 1/2 cups greens of choice
1 frozen banana
2 Tablespoons healthy fat
1/2 teaspoon green stevia powder
8-10 ice cubes

Place all ingredients in blender, and mix together until smooth. Serve.

NOTE: the fresh ginger will give this a hot little kick, and is great for most disease, related to inflammation. The exception is with skin irritations and rashes. They tend to do better when cinnamon is used instead, which will still help with inflammation, but isn't as likely to irritate sensitive skin.

peachy berry smoothie

1 cup water or LEMON TWIST
2 frozen peaches (pitted) - or PEACH'S N CREAM
SHERBET, or FRENCH VANILLA ICE CREAM
1/2 cup frozen strawberries
1 cup dark greens of choice
1 cup pineapple
1 scoop creamy vanilla protein powder or maca
root powder (optional)
2 Tablespoons healthy fat
1/2 teaspoon green stevia powder
8-10 ice cubes

peaches n cream milkshake

1 cup almond or coconut milk
1/4 cup GINGER ALE (optional) or 1/2" ginger root
2 frozen peaches (pitted)
1/2" fresh ginger root
1 cup fresh pineapple
1 scoop creamy vanilla protein powder, or maca
root powder
1/2 teaspoon pure vanilla extract
1/2 teaspoon stevia or other sweetener of choice
2 Tablespoons healthy fat of choice
8-10 ice cubes

old fashioned peachy shake

1 cup PEACH'S N CREAM SHERBET or 2 peaches (pitted)
1 cup QUICK KEIFER, MAGIC YOGURT, or FRENCH
VANILLA ICE CREAM
1/2 cup frozen pineapple chunks
1/2 cup water - filtered
1 /2 teaspoon stevia or other sweetener of choice

ALL ABOVE: Mix together in blender and serve.

tart cantaloupe
milkshake

1 cup non-dairy milk of choice
1/2 cup PINEAPPLE SPLASH (optional)
1 cup cantaloupe
1 cup fresh pineapple
1 scoop creamy vanilla protein or maca root powder
1 cup of greens (optional)
2 Tablespoons healthy fat
1/2 teaspoon green stevia powder
8-10 ice cubes
1/2 cup MAGIC YOGURT or KEFIR

Blend together and serve. If you'd like a swirl, stir in the magic yogurt or kefir just before serving.

www.naturesknockout.com

strawberry milkshake

I love this it's a quick treat, and so delicious!

1 cup coconut milk
1 cup MAGIC YOGURT, KEFIR or FRENCH VANILLA ICE CREAM
1 scoop creamy vanilla protein or maca root powder (optional)
4 pieces of ice
1/2 teaspoon green stevia powder
2 tablespoons healthy fat of choice
4-5 big frozen strawberries
Blend together until smooth, and serve.

www.naturesknockout.com

mint decadence
milkshake

If you love chocolate and mint, get ready for some yum! This is chocolatey rich and delicious!

2 1/2 cups almond or coconut milk
1 teaspoon vanilla extract
2 tablespoons raw cacao powder
1 tablespoon carob
1 tablespoon coconut oil
1 cup fresh greens of choice
1 banana or peeled apple
2 tablespoons raw honey or sweetener of choice
2 sprigs of fresh mint
1/2 cup walnuts or almonds (optional)

Blend ingredients together, except walnuts. Add nuts and pulse. Makes 2 servings. Cacao nibs are a great topper as well, for a chocolatey crunch.

70   www.naturesknockout.com

RAINBOW SMOOTHIES

for a special twist

Sometimes you just wanna kick back, and feel pampered. It's so fun, and easy to do, by blending your fruits separately from your smoothie. Here are some fun ideas to spark your creativity.

Or, if you're trying to entice kids or anyone afraid of healthy drinks, this is the best way to do it! Or take it a step further and make some fun, layered popsicles...now that is cool!

strawberry
slush

1 cup coconut milk
1/4 lime, peeled
1 tablespoon extra virgin olive oil
2 cups organic strawberries
1 teaspoon maca root powder (optional)
1 /2 teaspoon stevia or other sweetener of choice
6-8 ice cubes

Blend together and serve. If you'd like a swirl, stir in the magic yogurt or kefir just before serving.

mango & ginger shake

1 cup coconut milk
1 large mango, peeled and pitted
1/2 lime or 1/2 cup LIME DELIGHT
1 tablespoon coconut oil or healthy fat of choice
1/4-1/2" ginger root (depending upon thickness)
1 /2 teaspoon stevia or other sweetener of choice
8-10 ice cubes
1/2 cup MAGIC YOGURT or coconut milk kefir

Blend together and serve. If you'd like a swirl, stir in the magic yogurt or kefir just before serving. Add a tablespoon of MAGIC YOGURT, KEIFER or FRENCH VANILLA ICE CREAM.

www.naturesknockout.com

peaches n mint
swirl

1 cup water or PINEAPPLE PROBIOTIC juice
1 frozen banana
1/2 cup frozen peaches
1 tablespoon healthy fat
1/4 teaspoon stevia or other sweetener of choice
1-2 sprigs of fresh mint
8-10 ice cubes

Blend together the green smoothie portion. If you'd like a swirl, stir in 1/2 cup of any of our orange or peach colored shakes. Add a tablespoon of MAGIC YOGURT, KEIFER or FRENCH VANILLA ICE CREAM.

strawberry creamsicle
cooler

1/2 cup Orange Creamsicle Green Smoothie
1/2 cup Strawberry Cream Shake
1/4 cup Magic Yogurt or kefir

Stir the above recipes gently in a glass, then top with a tablespoon MAGIC YOGURT, KEIFER or FRENCH VANILLA ICE CREAM.

www.naturesknockout.com

strawberry basil
cream shake

1 cup coconut milk, or KEFIR
1 lime or LIME DELIGHT
1 tablespoon healthy fat of choice
1 cup organic strawberries
1/4 cup of fresh basil
1 /4 teaspoon stevia or other sweetener of choice
6-8 ice cubes

OPTIONAL: top with 1.2 cup MAGIC YOGURT, KEIFER or FRENCH VANILLA ICE CREAM

Blend together and serve. If you'd like a swirl, gently stir inMagic Yogurt or kefir just before serving.

www.naturesknockout.com

summer rainbow
refresher

Perfect on that hot summer day, or even a cold day that needs a little extra sunshine. Also a fun way treat for any special occasion feel a little more special!

1/3 cup Green Smoothie
1/3 cup Just Peachy Shake, or 2 frozen peaches
1/3 cup Strawberry Cream Shake or frozen strawberries

Blend together and serve. If you'd like a swirl, gently stir inMagic Yogurt or kefir just before serving.
OPTIONAL: top with MAGIC YOGURT, KEIFER or FRENCH VANILLA ICE CREAM.

The doctor of the future will no longer treat the human frame with drugs, but rather cure and prevent disease with nutrition –
Thomas Edison

VEGGIE

no sweets allowed

All of the drinks in this book are intended for transitioning to a more healthy eating, but these next few recipes are the very best for the ultimate health boost!

lime qyencher
cream smoothie

1 cup QUICK KEIFER or coconut milk
1/2 avocado
2 cups greens of choice
1 handful uncooked cabbage
1 lime or LIME DELIGHT
2 tablespoons healthy fat of choice
1 /4 teaspoon stevia or other sweetener of choice
8 ice cubes

Mix all ingredients in blender until smooth. Add ice and
pulse several times.

www.naturesknockout.com

A fit, healthy body is the best fashion statement — Jess C. Scott

chocoholic mint squeeze
1 cup QUICK KEIFER, MAGIC YOGURT, or nut milk
1/2 cup water
1 cup greens of choice
1/2 avocado
2-3 tablespoons raw cacao (or carob powder)
1/2 teaspoon stevia or other sweetener of choice
1-2 leaves of fresh mint
5 cubes ice

Mix all ingredients in blender until smooth

spiced veggie splash
3 large tomatoes, sliced
4 carrots
3 stalks celery
1 cup fresh greens of choice
1/4 green bell pepper
1/4 fresh beet
2 large sprigs of cilantro
1/8 sweet onion
2 cloves fresh garlic
1/2 teaspoon turmeric
1/4" slice of fresh ginger
1/4 teaspoon sea salt

Chop large vegetables into chunks, then place all ingredients in the blender. Mix until smooth.

italian lime
smoochie

1 cup water
1/4 cup lime delight (optional)
2 cups greens of choice
1 lime
1/2 fresh avocado meat
1 whole tomato
dash of sea salt (optional)
1 tablespoon Italian Seasoning Herbs

Mix all ingredients in blender until
smooth.

www.naturesknockout.com

*What you plant now, you will harvest later –
Og Mandino*

tomato-mango squeeze
2 fresh tomatoes
1 mango, pitted
1/2 cup QUICK KEIFER, MAGIC YOGURT or nut milk
1/2 cup cilantro
3 cups greens of choice
2 tablespoons lime juice, LIME DELIGHT or one of our probiotic juices
2 tablespoons healthy fat of choice

Chop large vegetables into chunks, then place all ingredients in the blender. Mix until smooth.

veggie 8
2 fresh tomatoes
1 fresh peach with skin
1 carrot
1 stalk celery
2 tablespoons lime juice, LIME DELIGHT or one of our probiotic juices
2 tablespoons healthy fat of choice

Chop large vegetables into chunks, then place all ingredients in the blender. Mix until smooth.

tomato with a kick
3 large tomatoes, sliced
1/4 cup chopped onion
2 stalks celery
1 bunch of cilantro
1 Tablespoon raw honey (optional)
2 tablespoons healthy fat of choice
1/2 teaspoon cumin powder
1/4 teaspoon sea salt
cayenne powder to taste
freshly ground pepper to taste

SHERBET

Delicious alone, or a great addition to any smoothie or shake!

pineapple peach sherbet

3 frozen pitted peaches
1 cup frozen pineapple or PINEAPPLE PROBIOTIC JUICE
1/2 teaspoon pure stevia
1/2 cup MAGIC YOGURT or nut milk

Blend until smooth and serve. Store in the freezer.

lime kiwi sherbet

4 cups kiwi (frozen)
1 fresh lime or LIME DELIGHT
1/2 teaspoon green stevia powder
enough water to get sherbet consistency

Blend until smooth and serve. Store in the freezer.

OLD FASHIONED ICE CREAMS

Any of these ice cream recipes, or our sherbets are great alone, or added into a smoothie for that perfect twist.

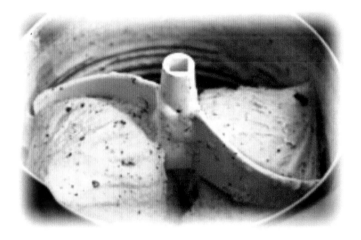

NOTE: For all of the old-fashioned ice creams, we recommend using canned coconut milk, as it contains binders.
We've used it with fresh coconut milk we make, but it tends to be more grainy or icy.

ANOTHER OPTION: You can use up to 1 Tablespoon of Guar Gum to fresh coconut milk, which will work as a binder. Just be sure to blend it well.

ALSO: We don't use xanthum gum for anything, as it is typically made with genetically modified *GMO" corn.

With the new day comes new strength and new thoughts —Eleanor Roosevelt

Churning ice cream was a tradition we enjoyed every Sunday in our household, so when we made our dietary changes, that was one of the hardest things to give up. But one day, I decided there had to be a way to make the most amazing raw ice creams that were all free of dairy, refined sugar, gluten, and soy. With absolute determination, I finally figured out how it could be done, and they were absolutely scrumptious!

french vanilla ice cream

4 cups rich coconut milk
3/4 cup raw honey
1 Tablespoon pure vanilla extract
1 Tablespoon maca root powder (optional)
1/2 teaspoon cinnamon (optional)
dash of sea salt

Blend until smooth and pour into the ice cream container of your ice cream freezer. Cover and place inside the Ice Cream Freezer. Alternate by adding ice and rock salt until the ice almost covers the lid of the container. Plug in the freezer and churn away for about 20 minutes. (This is a lighter ice cream than traditional and may not stop the freezer when done.) Eat right away, and any leftover can be stored in a freezer.

whipped cream

This is one of those very exciting accidents we fell upon, when we didn't have room in the freezer to put our ice cream maker with leftover ice cream in it. So we stuck the container in the refrigerator.
The next day, we found a glorious thing had taken place. The "French Vanilla Ice Cream" was a wonderful creation of whipped cream! It was delicious and kept that way for several days, refrigerated.
So we would recommend reserving some of the FRENCH VANILLA ICE CREAM, and placing it in the refrigerator after it has fully churned.
It's wonderful and contains NO CHEMICALS!! YAY!

butter cashew nut
ice cream

4 cups rich coconut milk
3/4 cup raw honey
1 Tablespoon pure vanilla extract
1 cup raw cashew pieces
2 tablespoons extra virgin olive oil
dash of sea salt

Blend until smooth and pour into the ice cream container of your
ice cream freezer. Cover and place inside the Ice Cream Freezer.
Alternate by adding ice and rock salt until the ice almost covers
the lid of the container. Plug in the freezer and churn away for
about 20 minutes. (This is a lighter ice cream than traditional and
may not stop the freezer when done.) Eat right away, and any
leftover can be stored in a freezer.

www.naturesknockout.com

cookie dough
ice cream

This is delicious with our raw macaroon cookie recipe or our chocolate chip cookie recipe in our "Beauty Bite Desserts Cookbook. "

4 cups rich coconut milk
3/4 cup raw honey
1 Tablespoon pure vanilla extract
1 Tablespoon maca root powder (optional)
1/2 teaspoon cinnamon (optional)
dash of sea salt

1 cup of cookie dough - add in the last 5 minutes of churning

Blend until smooth and pour into the ice cream container of your ice cream freezer. Cover and place inside the Ice Cream Freezer. Alternate by adding ice and rock salt until the ice almost covers the lid of the container. Plug in the freezer and churn away for about 20 minutes.

(This is a lighter ice cream than traditional and may not stop the freezer when done.) Eat right away, and any leftover can be stored in a freezer.

Remove lid from container and add the cookie dough in small chunks. Churn 5 more minutes, and serve.

www.naturesknockout.com

nutty coconut
ice cream

4 cups rich coconut milk
3/4 cup raw honey
1 Tablespoon pure vanilla extract
1/2 cup raw pecan pieces
1/2 cup raw walnuts, chopped
3/4 cup unsweetened coconut flakes
2 tablespoons extra virgin olive oil
dash of sea salt

Blend until smooth and pour into the ice cream container of your ice cream freezer. Cover and place inside the Ice Cream Freezer. Alternate by adding ice and rock salt until the ice almost covers the lid of the container. Plug in the freezer and churn away for about 20 minutes. (This is a lighter ice cream than traditional and may not stop the freezer when done.)

About 5 minutes before finishing, add the nuts and coconut flakes. Churn another 5 minutes, then serve. Eat right away, and any leftover can be stored in a freezer.

Mastering others is strength, mastering ourselves is true power – Lao Tsu

salted caramel
ice cream

4 cups rich coconut milk
1/3 cup raw honey
1/3 cup date sugar
1/4 cup coconut oil
1 Tablespoon pure vanilla extract
1 teaspoon lucuma powder (optional - adds nutrients & flavor)
1/2 teaspoon sea salt

Blend until smooth and pour into an ice cream container. Cover and place inside an Ice Cream Freezer. Alternate by adding ice and rock salt until the ice almost covers the lid of container. Plug in the freezer and churn away for about 20 minutes. (This is a lighter ice cream than traditional and may not stop the freezer when done.) Eat right away, and any leftover can be stored in a freezer.

Be happy for this moment, this moment is your life
— Omar Khayyam

caramel pecan
ice cream

4 cups rich coconut milk
1/2 cup raw honey
1/4 cup date sugar
1 Tablespoon pure vanilla extract
1 Tablespoon maca root powder (optional)
dash of sea salt
1 cup pecan pieces - add in last 5 minutes of churning

Blend until smooth and pour into an ice cream container. Cover and place inside an Ice Cream Freezer. Alternate by adding ice and rock salt until the ice almost covers the lid of container. Plug in the freezer and churn away for about 20 minutes. (This is a lighter ice cream than traditional and may not stop the freezer when done.)

Remove lid and stir in pecan pieces. Churn 5 more minutes.

Eat right away, and any leftover can be stored in a freezer.

mint chocolate chip
ice cream

4 cups rich coconut milk
3/4 cup raw honey
1 teaspoon pure vanilla extract
1 cup fresh mint leaves or 1 teaspoon peppermint extract
1/3 cup raw spinach leaves
dash of sea salt
1 cup raw cacao nibs

Blend all ingredients together until smooth and pour into the ice cream container of your ice cream freezer. Cover and place inside the Ice Cream Freezer. Alternate by adding ice and rock salt until the ice almost covers the lid of the container. Plug in the freezer and churn away for about 20 minutes. In the last 5-10 minutes of freezing, add cacao nibs. (This is a lighter ice cream than traditional and may not stop the freezer when done.) Eat right away, and any leftover can be stored in a freezer.

www.naturesknockout.com

pistachio
ice cream

4 cups rich coconut milk
3/4 cup raw honey
1/2 teaspoon pure almond extract
1/3 cup organic spinach leaves
dash of sea salt

1 1/2 cups raw pistachios, shelled - add 1 cup in the last 5 minutes of freezing

Blend until smooth and pour into the ice cream container of your ice cream freezer. Cover and place inside the Ice Cream Freezer. Alternate by adding ice and rock salt until the ice almost covers the lid of the container. Plug in the freezer and churn away for about 20 minutes. (This is a lighter ice cream than traditional and may not stop the freezer when done.)

Add 1 cup of the pistachios in the last 5 minutes of freezing. Churn and serve. Eat right away, and any leftover can be stored in a freezer.

Garnish with the remaining pistachios, if desired.

chocolate lovers ice cream

4 cups rich coconut milk
3/4 cup raw honey
3/4 - 1 cup raw cacao (or carob) powder
1 Tablespoon pure vanilla extract
1 Tablespoon maca root powder (optional)
dash of sea salt

1/2 cup cacao nibs - optional

Blend until smooth and pour into the ice cream container of your ice cream freezer. Cover and place inside the Ice Cream Freezer. Alternate by adding ice and rock salt until the ice almost covers the lid of the container. Plug in the freezer and churn away for about 20 minutes. (This is a lighter ice cream than traditional and may not stop the freezer when done.) Eat right away, and any leftover can be stored in a freezer.

Place cacao nibs with mostly frozen ice cream, about 10 minutes before finishing. Churn 10 minutes and serve. Garnish with a cacao nibs if desired.

german chocolate
ice cream

4 cups rich coconut milk
3/4 cup raw honey (reserve 1/4 cup, set aside)
3/4 cup raw cacao (or carob) powder
1 Tablespoon pure vanilla extract
dash of sea salt

raw honey -reserved
1/2 cup unsweetened dry coconut flakes
1 cup chopped walnuts or pecans

Blend until smooth and pour into the ice cream container of your ice cream freezer. Cover and place inside the Ice Cream Freezer. Alternate by adding ice and rock salt until the ice almost covers the lid of the container. Plug in the freezer and churn away for about 20 minutes. (This is a lighter ice cream than traditional and may not stop the freezer when done.)

About 5 minutes before finishing, add the remaining 1/4 cup of raw honey, coconut flakes, and nuts. Continue churning 5 minutes, then serve.

Eat right away, and any leftover can be stored in a freezer.

OPTIONAL-Garnish with more coconut, nuts, and drizzle with raw honey.

lemon squeeze ice cream

4 cups rich coconut milk
3/4 cup raw honey
2/3 cup fresh lemon juice
1 tablespoon fresh lemon zest
dash of sea salt

Place all ingredients together in the blender until smooth. Pour into an ice cream freezer and use as directed. Churn about 30 minutes. Remove from the freezer and serve, or use in green smoothies for a wonderful tangy texture.

Add 1 tablespoon lemon zest for a garnish if desired.

old fashioned peach
ice cream

4 cups rich coconut milk
3/4 cup raw honey
2/3 cup fresh lemon juice
dash of ginger

1 large peach - blend and reserve until ice cream is mostly frozen

Place all ingredients together in the blender until smooth. Pour into an ice cream freezer and use as directed. Churn about 30 minutes. Remove from the freezer and serve, or use in green smoothies for a wonderful tangy texture.

About 10 minutes early, remove lid and stir in the blended peach. Freeze 10 more minutes and serve.

www.naturesknockout.com

BONUS SIPS

horchata

We love horchata, so this may be a little bit of a selfish pleasure--but we think you'll love this delicious cooler with a perfect south of the border flavor as well. Let us know how you like it! :)

1 cup brown rice - raw (for a grain free twist, use shredded coconut)
5 cups water - filtered
3/4 cup coconut milk
2 teaspoons pure vanilla extract
1 Tablespoon ground cinnamon
1/2 teaspoon stevia powder

Place rice and water in blender and mix 30 seconds. Pour into a pitcher. Let set 4 hours.
Place a nut milk bag on a pitcher, and strain the rice, squeezing out all extra water. Mix in all of the remaining ingredients and chill. Serve over chopped ice.

All our dreams can come true–if we have the courage to pursue them. – Walt Disney

FOREVER YOUNG TEA

ginger cinnamon

Ginger and cinnamon are both rich in anti-inflammatory properties, which makes this tea an especially beneficial beverage during flu and cold season as well.

1 cups warm water
2 tablespoons raw honey
1 drop ginger therapeutic grade essential oil
1/2 teaspoon ground cinnamon
Mix together and serve.

www.naturesknockout.com

GREEN SMOOTHIES INCOGNITO

Green smoothie popsicles:

Simply pour leftover smoothie into ice cube trays or popsicle molds and freeze.

Green smoothie fruit leather:

Pour onto non-stick dehydrator trays. Turn temperature to 105 Degrees and dry until leathery consistency. When dry on top, turn over and place on regular tray until finished.

CHOCOLATE XO

hot chocolate
1/4 cup warm water
1 1/2 tablespoons raw cacao powder
3 tablespoons date or coconut sugar
1/2 cup almond or rice milk
1/4 teaspoon pure vanilla extract or cinnamon
Boil water on stovetop.
Mix remaining ingredients together and pour in boiling water, which will warm everything.

For an extra treat, top with a spoonful of COCONUT MILK ICE CREAM or COCONUT CREAM or from our Beauty In Every Bite Desserts Cookbook

hot chocolate mint
1/2 cup water
3 tablespoons raw cacao powder
4 pitted dates or 3 Tablespoons date sugar
1/2 cup coconut milk
1/2 teaspoon pure vanilla extract or cinnamon
sprig or two of fresh peppermint leaves

Place all ingredients in a blender and mix 4 minutes until hot.

For an extra treat, top with a spoonful of COCONUT MILK ICE CREAM or COCONUT CREAM or from our Beauty In Every Bite Desserts Cookbook

vegan
chocolate milk

1 cup creamy coconut milk
1 1/2 tablespoons raw cacao powder
1 1/2 tablespoons raw honey
1/4 teaspoon pure vanilla extract or cinnamon (optional)

Mix remaining ingredients together in a mini blender until mixed well and frothy.

For an extra treat, top with a spoonful of COCONUT MILK ICE CREAM or COCONUT CREAM or from our Beauty In Every Bite Desserts Cookbook

INTERNATIONAL COOKING

We love our blog followers and the fact that they come from all over the world. Here is a simple conversion chart

liquid equivalents & conversions

capacity

weight

1 cup	8 fl. oz.	1/2 pint	237 ml.
2 cups	16 fl. oz.	1 pint	474 ml.
4 cups	32 fl. oz	1 quart	946 ml.
2 pints	32 fl. oz.	1 quart	0.964 liters
4 quarts	128 fl. oz.	1 gallon	3.784 liters
dash	less than 1/8 teaspoon		

dry equivalents & conversions

capacity

weight

3 teaspoons	1 tablespoon	1/2 ounce	14.3 grams
2 tablespoons	1/8 cup	1 ounce	28.3 grams
4 tablespoons	1/4 cup	2 ounces	56.7 grams
5 1/3 tablespoons	1/3 cup	2.6 ounces	75.6 grams
8 tablespoons	1/2 cup	4 ounces	113.4 grams
32 tablespoons	2 cups	16 oz. (1lb.)	453.6 grams
64 tablespoons	4 cups	32 oz. (2 lb.)	907 grams

www.naturesknockout.com

THAT'S A WRAP!

OR is it... just the beginning?

We're used to working until we hear those 3 precious words, "that's a wrap!" So it seemed like the appropriate way to end this book. Although, we hardly see what we're sharing here as an ending at all.

Our hope is that it will spark the greatest new beginning in your life, one that will excite and give you hope for something so much greater than you've ever had before. Even if you're like me, and started out thinking you were pretty healthy, I believe that you're in for some wonderful surprises as you embark on this incredible transformation!

Enjoy these amazing recipes that we share with full hearts, overflowing in gratitude. We feel so truly blessed for the things we've learned, the health it has brought us, and for the opportunities we have to share. Continue to enjoy many more recipes and tips on our website, www.naturesknockout.com, and we've got a lot more books, CD's and videos coming your way!

We wish we could reach out and hug you, but since we can't, please consider yourself hugged! You are wonderful and we wish you the very best in your quest to look and feel beautiful!

xox

laurie & tiffany

table of contents

www.naturesknockout.com

www.naturesknockout.com

CPSIA information can be obtained
at www.ICGtesting.com
Printed in the USA
LVXC01n2232151213
365469LV00015B/145